gratitude♡reflections

A GUIDED JOURNAL
FOR CULTIVATING PEACE
AND PRESENCE

GEMMA FARRELL

Gratitude Reflections

Published by Accelerator Books.

For information, please contact Accelerator Books, P.O. Box 1241, Princeton, NJ 08542.

Designed by Eve Siegel Designs.
Typeset by TypeWriting.
Cover photo by Bahman Farzad.

ISBN: 978-0-9841399-2-7

INTRODUCTION

This guided journal offers a series of reflections that are meant to mirror the gratitude, generosity, and understanding that bring a sense of peace and presence to your daily life. Whether you choose to make daily journal entries, fill in a whole bunch of pages all at once, or just explore these reflections from time to time, I hope that the thoughts shared in this book prompt you to discover the compassion and understanding that reside in your own heart.

We all long to create more meaningful relationships with others, with ourselves, and with our life circumstances. When we lift those relationships up, through even the simplest practices, such as a meditative walk or some deep breaths or a series of Sun Salutations, we gain focus and fortitude, and we remind ourselves of what truly matters. What relationships do you want to lift up in your practice today?

Our freedom lies in our willingness to allow others to disappoint us. Resentment keeps us trapped. We are free only when we meet our disappointments with a forgiving heart. Who and what in your life need your forgiveness?

We all want to be at peace with ourselves and at ease with any given moment, just as it is. And beyond that, most of us long to unfold, to open ourselves to others in an authentic, intimate way. What keeps you closed?

We cultivate awareness when we touch our experience with our full presence. Throughout the day, ask yourself: What am I doing right now? In this moment, how can I show up more fully and approach what I am feeling with a quiet attentiveness?

Take time today to feel the freshness of nature, even if you just step outside for a few minutes to experience the air on your skin or to look at the sky. When we pause to appreciate the beauty of this natural world, we develop deeper gratitude for the magnificence that surrounds us.

Look for the beauty that lives within you. Recognizing yourself as a miraculous entity, filled with magic and mystery, you awaken to a sense of wonder at the gift of this life. Which people and what activities help you to remember your inner beauty?

REFLECTION
7

If we could trust that the people in our lives are essential to our emotional and spiritual growth, we would try to love everyone who has been put on our path, even if for now we sometimes wish they weren't there. If we believe we are in their lives because they need our love, then our only choice is to open our hearts.

Rather than resisting uncertainty, can you engage it in a playful way and let life surprise you? There is a great deal of freedom in trusting that you don't have to know what's coming next.

Take some time, even just a few minutes, to stretch and move in a way that lets you discover more of your body's inner landscape rather than just its outer form. When we are genuinely curious about our physical bodies, it is possible to let some of the self-criticism fall away. How can you practice being less self-critical and more self-curious?

May my thoughts arise from a joyful mind that perceives the beauty in every encounter. May I encounter myself with that same joyful mind.

When you listen attentively to the voice of truth within, you cultivate your own personal wisdom. What do you need to do to quiet the outer voices of popular culture and social media so that you can hear your inner guidance?

Are you willing to make a conscious effort to be more accepting of your imperfections? If you can learn to embrace your imperfections, you will naturally become more tolerant of others as well. In any given day, you receive countless invitations to foster self-acceptance. What are the qualities you struggle to accept about yourself? Can you turn toward yourself with gentleness and see how that softens your heart toward others, too?

Your words possess incredible power. How can you speak in a way that promotes peace? Bringing awareness to your speech generates an atmosphere of gentleness and ease, which is a blessing to everyone around you.

It takes courage to recognize that we have never been here before, that our hearts and minds have never touched this precise moment. We may have been in this place, at this same time of day, hundreds or thousands of times, but we have not experienced the newness of this moment before now, nor will we ever have the chance to experience it again. What does it feel like to have the courage to meet the present moment and recognize its precious, ephemeral beauty?

We are so much more expansive than we tend to believe. We could all use a stretching routine that keeps us a little more flexible in our bodies, our minds, and our hearts. How can you extend yourself beyond your critical thoughts, limited beliefs, self-doubt, and distrust of others? What keeps you feeling tight and closed off from yourself and other people?

REFLECTION
16

One of the most valuable gifts of a regular meditation practice is the chance to develop patience. It requires some patience to stay with your emotions as they arise, even when you want to run away. Would you be willing to sit quietly and observe your emotions for a few minutes either when you first wake up or just before you go to sleep?

Sometimes self-reflection puts us in contact with parts of ourselves that feel broken. We might wonder why we bother if it only makes us feel worse. This is where trust comes in. It is possible to see beyond what feels broken inside and know that you are already whole. But you need to trust in that truth, especially when the brokenness can feel so real.

One of the best recipes for happiness is to focus on what you already have rather than on what you think you want. We have already been given so much. Do you tend to become preoccupied with ideas about what you think you need to be happy? For a few moments, allow your thoughts to rest on what is already here, and let yourself be filled with gratitude.

A spirit of devotion colors our world in the softest hues and makes all of the circumstances of our lives – however painful – somehow lovely. Do you feel a desire to serve something bigger than yourself? Do you wish to nurture that desire? What would that look like?

Close your eyes and imagine holding yourself with tenderness and loving kindness. What is it like to be cradled in compassion? Could you make it a practice to do this for yourself and for the people you care about?

There is a lovely Buddhist prayer: "May I become at all times, both now and forever, a bridge for those with rivers to cross . . . a servant to those in need." Pretty much everyone we know has rivers to cross. Everyone is in need of love. If we ever feel lost or without purpose, here is our call to action. We can be a bridge in even the smallest of ways: in a simple conversation, in the way our eyes meet another's. We can serve in countless unseen but very real ways.

Inner awareness is like background music. If you listen closely, you can catch the strain of a melody that is always present, its soft rhythm just waiting for you to fall in and let the dance of life lead you to places you did not even realize were there. Are you listening?

When you come face-to-face with the shortcomings of those you care for deeply, genuine compassion breathes its first breath. It is easy to feel kindness toward those who we already admire and appreciate. But real compassion is born when we begin to move past resentment toward someone who has hurt us. May we seek opportunities to celebrate the birth of genuine loving kindness.

When we embrace a new perspective, rather than letting it make us feel isolated or separated from others, we have the chance to say: "I have received the incredible gift of a profound new way of seeing myself and the world around me. It is my deepest wish that this new perspective be born in you as well."

We have so little time to treasure the presence of each other. If you are someone's mother or someone's child, someone's brother or someone's sister, if you are someone's father or someone's friend, you have to let them know how precious they are to you. Everyone longs to be told that they are cherished and held close. Who can you tell today?

The body is a temple – a place of praise, a place of solace, a place of peace, a place of pilgrimage. How can you choose to honor your body today?

We have so little time to cherish the ones we love and learn to love the ones we don't cherish yet. What would it be like to open your heart to whomever you find yourself with today? If you love them, cherish them. If you don't love them yet, how can you start?

If we can make room for suffering – our own and that of others –
we will see that there is enough space for pain to coexist alongside
pleasure and for sorrow to settle snugly into the contours of joy. It
is not that we need to eliminate one to accommodate the other but
rather that we can broaden the field of our awareness to encompass
both. Notice when you push away discomfort, and see if you can
make some room for it instead.

Our hearts are expansive enough to include the totality of our life experience. This is what allows our compassion to flourish. It is exactly this sort of openheartedness that will serve us and the people we encounter in our day-to-day walk toward wisdom. How can you expand your heart?

Each of us is devoted to something. What is the current object of your devotion? Your parents? Your work? Your studies? Your children? Your romantic partner? Your self-image? Your God?

A common spiritual metaphor likens the mind to a mirror that reflects our true essence. Our work is to clear the mirror of the dust of doubt, insecurity, fear, ignorance, and misunderstanding that accumulates on its surface. What is obscuring your vision of who you really are?

The magnitude of suffering in the world can be staggering, But becoming overwhelmed in the face of suffering actually hinders the loving kindness we want to cultivate. This is why it seems important to generate equanimity. With a heart that is balanced and even, we can find an inner sense of ease and an ability to hold ourselves steady in the face of tragedy and loss so that we can be a source of peace and healing for ourselves and others. What could you do to foster a genuine sense of equanimity?

Knowing that all things arise and pass away, may we be calm and open, willing to embrace all of life with generosity. There is absolutely nothing that lasts forever, and holding on too tightly only constricts the heart and makes it smaller.

What would it be like to see everyone as our sisters and brothers? Every encounter would feel like a family reunion.

We need to develop a flexible vision, with the capacity to see both near and far, up close and at a distance. Sometimes we require a narrow focus, and at other times we have to pan way back and take in the breadth of experience from an open perspective.

It is such an immense privilege to awaken to our capacity – as individuals and as a community – to uplift and heal others. Together we can make a profound difference for our community, both nearby and further away. As Rumi wrote, "Our friendship is made of being awake."

Generosity flows from the recognition that there are infinite possibilities for how our lives could unfold. We might meet the challenge of a grave illness or a catastrophic accident, or we might experience the betrayal of a friend, the loss of a love, the decline of a parent or the illness of a child, or the strain of financial hardship. And yet somehow grace carries us through the bleak terrain and becomes the birthplace of generosity.

The thing is, we don't always get to choose the difficulties we encounter. But recognizing the grace that holds us, and responding with humility whenever and wherever we can, is always a choice we can embrace.

None of us wants to end up grieving for an unlived life. Each moment invites us to live fully and wholeheartedly, with the wide-eyed wonder and excitement of a child.

We tend to separate our idea of work from the essence of our being. Work is something to get over with so that we can enjoy our lives. But when we separate our work like that, we decline one of life's greatest invitations: to unite our labor with our love. How can you make your work a genuine expression of love?

May I see in a way that recognizes the truth in everyone I meet.
May I meet myself with that same pure vision.

In *The Prophet*, Kahlil Gibran entreats: "Let your bending in the archer's hand be for gladness." Even our healthiest, most loving relationships ask us to yield to the other. May we experience the immense joy that comes with bending for those we love.

When we meet the present moment without judgment, the door of peace swings wide open, and we step into the spaciousness that welcomes all that is.

My friend has a piece of advice she recites often: "Open your hands, and let it go." Whatever is plaguing you, whatever is weighing you down, whatever it is that troubles you – open your hands. What are you holding onto too tightly? How can you let it go?

It is not so much that peace is elusive but rather that uncertainty is so very persistent. Sometimes we know that peace is just within reach. But the pull of doubt can be awfully strong. What is standing in the way of your connection to the inner peace that is always there?

When we allow our work to be illuminated by the fire of our love, our work can become an expression of our care and concern for the sacred mystery that lives within and all around us. When love illuminates our work, our work becomes the instrument through which we play our own unique heart song.

Contentment is quiet and modest, while insecurity can be so much louder and more tenacious. Our fears and uncertainties call to us constantly. It's no wonder we have trouble hearing the peace that speaks in the silence. What voice are you attuned to, and how can you amplify the call of contentment?

Deep, inner happiness rests in our willingness to let things be and to resist the unrelenting desire to change people or circumstances. Most of all, happiness depends on our capacity to shore up against the eroding need to improve ourselves. The relentless quest for self-improvement robs us of quietude and, ultimately, kills our joy. What could you "let be" today?

REFLECTION
49

What if we could purify our hearts of the critical thoughts that limit our fullest expression of loving kindness? As the barriers of self-judgment dissolve, we are free to radiate love in all directions, unimpeded by the limitations of a small sense of self.

We all search for refuge – a place of calm, safety, warmth, and connection. Most of the time we find ourselves just outside the door, caught up in the busyness of doing. Whenever we respond to our experience with tenderness and love, we step inside the shelter of pure awareness.

To be responsible literally means to be "able to respond." To respond, rather than to react. It is possible to change our reactive patterns with consistent practice. When we accept that responsibility, we become more readily able to respond thoughtfully, mindfully, and even lovingly.

Every time we are able to arrive more completely in the here and now, we encounter ourselves anew. Each of these conscious moments is a reunion with our innermost self.

Genuine service means that we open ourselves to give whatever we can, whenever and wherever we can. Service is a gift that we give in each moment, in ways both big and small. What are the gifts you can offer right now?

The Zen Buddhist tradition has a wonderful way of describing the shift from a focus on the foreground of experience to an awareness of the background that is always and ever present. They call this shift "the backward step." How can you step back this week and rest in open awareness?

Mythologist Joseph Campbell said, "The privilege of a lifetime is to be who you are." Who are you in your innermost nature, and how can you embody the tremendous privilege of being fully and wholly yourself?

Both contentment and fear – opposites though they may be – are faithful, enduring companions. It's just that we are more attuned to the voice of fear. We need to listen more carefully for the shy whisper of contentment, patiently waiting in the background of our days.

Neuroscientists are proving that just a few weeks of consistent mindfulness practice develops the compassion centers of the brain, reduces negativity, and increases emotional balance. Could you dedicate ten minutes each day to a mindfulness meditation practice to expand your capacity for self-acceptance and unconditional love and manifest the pure, inclusive loving kindness of which we are all capable?

To be a servant, we have to be willing to surrender our agenda. If we are holding too tightly to our idea of how serving should look, we have already gotten in our own way, and the path of sincere, heartfelt service will begin to disappear before us. Before we know it, we will find ourselves lost in the small, tight tangle of self-doubt. To stay on track, we have to keep asking: "What does she need? How can I help him? Where can I share love and care?"

By a complex confluence of circumstances, we have landed here –
with our relationships, material security, and sense of safety relatively
intact. May we recognize the miracle inherent in the fact that we can
say, "All is well."

May we be willing to be blinded by gratitude so that we no longer see what we want but rather what we have so that we cannot even think of what to ask for because there is so much to be thankful for.

A true friend is someone who sees past your faults and straight into the essence of who you are. Our practice is about learning to be that kind of friend to ourselves.

A wish for today: May my steps be light and gentle. May I walk in peace. You might even choose to recite these words to yourself as you do a brief walking meditation, taking slow, relaxed steps, mindful of your breath.

We are capable of living at any point on the wide spectrum of physical experience. Illness or injury can confine us to a limited range of slow movement. We might be racing with anxiety or paralyzed by psychological pain. The human spirit can accommodate all manner of challenge. Wherever we find ourselves on the spectrum, we can dedicate all of our actions – big or small, quick or slow – to a higher purpose.

Recently, a friend shared her fear that her spiritual growth had created distance in many of her relationships. Ironically, the more spiritually evolved she became, the more difficult it was for her to relate to family and friends whose values now appeared so shallow. Here is where our spiritual work gains traction and we can begin to put our learning into practice.

The most powerful thing we can do is to send love out to those who are struggling. We do not need an advanced degree or an impressive résumé to do that. We do not need to be clever or wealthy or good-looking or different from anyone else. We just need to know that everyone is struggling in some way and to send them love.

With humility, from the simplicity of your innermost essence, you can become a vehicle for the ultimate power to come through you: the power to change yourself, to change others, and to change the world through love.

The root of gratitude is the recognition that things could always be worse – that they are indeed worse for many people. There is so much that we take for granted and so many ways in which we can share from the abundance of our own good fortune.

Everything that leads to spiritual depth – the study of sacred Scripture, an understanding of profound spiritual teachings, the grappling with conceptual frameworks, and self-exploration – is in preparation for the birth of compassion. We can feel compassion take form and grow within us, nourished by the wisdom and insights we take in and strengthened by our own personal practices.

We do not know what might be happening for someone. At any given moment, a person might be receiving devastating news, falling deeply in love, facing some inner demon, sinking into apathy, flailing in confusion, or realizing a profound truth. It's never a bad idea to hold such a person in our hearts and lift him or her up.

Humility expresses itself in the desire to connect to oneness, dissolve the sense of separation between ourselves and others, and allow the feeling of an all-pervading unity to infuse our entire being. If we can stay in contact with this connectedness, it keeps us humble and makes others' happiness as valuable as our own.

Dancers take a bow at the end of their performance. After all, they spent hours perfecting its execution, and the audience is applauding their effort and dedication. But when we live a life of devotion, we do not feel as though we are performing the dance. We believe that the dance comes through us. And when we bow, we bow to the spirit that moves within all of us and to the beauty of this shared dance we call life.

If you have ever witnessed someone walking the path of service with honesty and humility, then you have seen firsthand what a profound blessing it is to serve.

A Bodhisattva is a person who is able to reach enlightenment but delays doing so out of compassion so as to save suffering beings. The essence of Bodhisattva wisdom is to cherish others more than oneself. Imagine holding others so dear that their well-being is as important as your own. You might catch a glimpse of that possibility if you consider someone you already care for deeply: your child, your partner, your parent, or your closest friend. From there, you can embark on a lifelong practice of learning to cherish everyone else in that way.

There are far too many people and not nearly enough time. We have to try to make every word an expression of kindness, every act a sign of love.

Tara Brach teaches a Buddhist technique called RAIN, from the acronym R for "Recognize what is happening," A for "Allow for things to be as they are," I for "Investigate with intimate awareness," N for "Nonidentification" – try not to identify with whatever is arising. RAIN provides a straightforward format for a mindfulness practice in which you approach your present-moment experience with curiosity and compassion. Notice what comes up for you as you engage in this technique for a few minutes.

Notice your thoughts. Then let them go – and notice some more thoughts. That's all.

Service has the inestimable benefit of dissolving the delusion of separateness. From a place of humility, the desire to serve another arises with the understanding that we are inextricably connected and that we all wish for true peace and inner joy.

We have the privilege of this life on Earth, and there is no time to lose. If we want to move forward on the spiritual path, we must make the most of our experiences in this lifetime to awaken to the deeper truth of our oneness with all beings. In *The Way of the Bodhisattva*, Shantideva advises: "Take advantage of this human boat. Free yourself from sorrow's mighty stream."

Happiness is to some degree a matter of perspective – a way of seeing the world. We cannot always change our circumstances, but we always have the choice to change our perspective. Through the eyes of gratitude, happiness comes into clearer focus.

80

May whatever you meet today be an opportunity to develop an intelligent heart and a compassionate mind, a forgiving vision and a healing voice, tender hands and strong spirit.

We are always practicing something. Like musicians, athletes, artists, and academics who practice for countless hours, our thoughts, words, and actions are constantly refining our skills. You can become adept at one-upmanship, skilled at hiding your true feelings, excellent at wielding anger. Or you can choose, with every breath, to develop generosity, kindness, honesty, and compassion.

Loving service is the real deal, and the currency is love itself. Can you feel your heart expand when you consider the concrete ways in which you can serve?

We all reach for certainty and security. We want to figure things out, get them to where we want them to be, and then keep them there. We tend to lose sight of the fact that everything is always shifting and that instead of trying to keep things static, we could choose to rest in the pure awareness that lies beyond the changing landscapes of our relationships, our careers, and our physical bodies.

Have you ever noticed how quick you are to blame someone as soon as things aren't going the way you want them to? It is almost second nature to find someone to blame – often that someone is yourself. Blaming can feel empowering: it can be liberating to focus our sadness, anger, or resentment on a particular target. But blame is never as good as forgiveness. There is no healing in blame, and rather than soothing the pain, it only makes it worse. Forgiveness is the best remedy, and there is nothing more healing than the balm of love.

Prayer does not have to be formulaic, ritualized, or dogmatic. In its purest form, prayer is an expression of love itself. Whenever you feel love expand from inside, you are praying with your entire being.

Life is more than a series of tasks you get done so that you can move on to the next thing. If we are always trying to get things done, we cannot be fully present to whatever is happening right now. How can you slow down and give your full attention to the present moment?

You can use your breath to dive deeper into spiritual awareness. Take a deep breath, and pause at the top of your inhalation. Exhale completely, and pause at the bottom of your exhalation. In the spaces between the in-breath and the out-breath, we come into closer contact with the eternal essence that is always there.

We are always surrounded by infinite, unconditional love. Grace equips us to become a channel for expressing that limitless love in a more finite way. When we see our relationships in the context of grace, it becomes easier to forgive, easier to accept, and easier to love.

There is a wonderful quote from Andy Warhol: "Most people have trouble with love – always wanting the other person to be a soufflé that never falls." If we get the temperature and the timing just right, we can create a perfect soufflé. But it is the nature of a soufflé to fall, and it is the nature of relationships to change shape.

178 Gratitude Reflections

The idea of having a mindfulness practice is to bring the spirit of mindfulness to your entire day. If you practice mindfulness for even a few minutes, the energy it generates can expand to fill all the hours of your day. If you feel a sense of joy or gratitude, that feeling can color all the other moments in your day. This is why we practice in the first place so that we can take the feeling tone that our practice creates and bring it with us to all the circumstance we encounter.

"Devotion" is defined in the dictionary as "love, loyalty, or enthusiasm for a person, activity, or cause." The good news is that we are creatures of devotion with an intense impulse to love, deep leanings toward loyalty, and a strong tendency toward enthusiasm. When we harness this spirit of devotion, it can guide our actions toward compassion and understanding.

Conscious breathing is one of the simplest and most effective tools for raising awareness and fostering a more authentic presence. Zen Buddhist teacher Thich Nhat Hanh says, "Breathing in, you know you are breathing in. Breathing out, you know you are breathing out." It really is that simple. Turning your attention to your breathing creates the possibility of being more present in each moment so that you can enjoy its wonders and its beauty.

Radhanath Swami shares a teaching that suggests that we cultivate the qualities of a chicken. A chicken will peck through a pile of garbage to find food and leave the rest aside. Like a chicken, we should look for the best qualities in others and disregard the rest. In your encounters today, consciously dwell on the positive qualities of the people you engage with, and give less attention to their shortcomings. This could be the recipe for a wonderful day.

True love requires understanding. If you really try to understand someone, you will find it much easier to love him, and your understanding will help you to love him better. If you want to love well, you must seek to understand the other person first. Then you will know what she needs, what makes her happy, what causes her suffering, and you can love in a way that truly contributes to her well-being.

Ultimately, the spiritual path is a solitary one: your own personal, private walk. In a spirit of solitude, seek to touch your experience with humility and honesty. Insight and understanding unfold personally and uniquely in your innermost heart.

REFLECTION
96

If you can make time to rest in pure awareness – always most accessible in stillness and silence – you may sense the presence of grace within and around you. Touching that presence in a quiet and honest way every day breathes life into an inner relationship that will accompany you throughout your days and nights.

The particulars of your life may be less important than you might think. It seems that if you follow the compass of your own heart and orient yourself in the direction of love and kindness, you are bound to end up where you are supposed to be.

One of the best responses to feeling misunderstood is to try to understand the other person. If someone misunderstands you, it is because something is preventing him from seeing your truth and your basic goodness. It is less important to be understood than it is to understand.

Our days are rife with distractions; many things take our thoughts in myriad directions. We need a place to land, a familiar place to return to time again throughout the day so that we do not find ourselves lost in mindless wanderings. When you are still, even just for a few breaths, your mind can rest in quietude, and after a while, that peaceful place becomes more familiar and easier to reach again when you get off track.

May my heart expand to hold all of the people around me in the warm light of love. May I hold myself in that same expansive heart.

ABOUT THE AUTHOR

Gemma Farrell teaches yoga, meditation, mindfulness, and other spiritual practices at Gratitude Yoga in Princeton, NJ. She is inspired to share practices that open our hearts in a spirit of devotion and loving service.

Also by Gemma Farrell: *Gratitude Cleanse: 21 Days to Cleanse Your Body, Open Your Mind, and Awaken Your Heart.*

www.ingramcontent.com/pod-product-compliance
Lightning Source LLC
Chambersburg PA
CBHW060757100426
42813CB00004B/858